Tendering the Body

poems by

Brittany Brewer

Finishing Line Press
Georgetown, Kentucky

Tendering the Body

ACKNOWLEDGMENTS

Grey Coven Publishing: In seeking compassion/ Ace of cups, Reversed, My spirit
wants/ The lovers
Hole in the Head Review: The girls I grew up with were slick, The store is closed now
Months to Years: Loss upon returning home from visiting the Adirondacks with
friends
Rougarou: A Journal of Arts and Literature: New England Secrets, When I storytell
myself
Wild Roof Journal: Towards softness

I am deeply appreciative to the above journals and editors who have provided space
to several of these poems previously, some in different iterations. Additionally, I am
also incredibly grateful to those who have supported me in this artmaking journey,
from the folks who offered feedback on poems to those who offered love and care,
especially my advisor, Janine; my parents, Ross & Darlene; my Aunt Tammy; my
found family (you know who you are), and my spouse, Steve.

Publisher: Leah Huete de Maines
Editor: Christen Kincaid
Cover Art: Audrey Gallagher www.audreyelizaphoto.com
Author Photo: Steve Graham
Cover Design: Elizabeth Maines McCleavy

Order online: www.finishinglinepress.com
also available on amazon.com

Author inquiries and mail orders:
Finishing Line Press
PO Box 1626
Georgetown, Kentucky 40324
USA

Contents

When I storytell myself

I want to say that the Midwest does not live in my body—instead I share that I was pulled from state to state five times before I was twelve. I share the first choice that was mine was to leave, to move to a city over ten times the population of smalltown, Indiana, known as home to the company that supplied Michael Jackson's casket and—unironically teenage—we declared the town slogan should be, "Everyone is dying to live here." From twelve to twenty-one I was saturated in a Midwest state of mind, I felt heavy, uncertain. The only thing I knew for sure was that I wanted to inhabit a space that was bigger than me, where there were so many people moving and being that I could disappear, that I could slip out of the strange skin I had donned by default and slide into another, experimenting in and out and around bodies in order to find my own footing. I did this urgently. I scrambled to subsume myself in order to seek some kind of clarity, running from 6,000 towards 80,000 towards 178,000 towards 1.8 million in search of the safety promised by different bodies, by more bodies. And each time, I want to say that I came closer to knowing myself. I want to say that I had grown more expansive, more queer, more pleasure-seeking than my midwest self could stand to contain. I want to say that it's easy, being back, that when I walk down these new smalltown streets in this different midwestern town, that I feel safe. But still, I find it hard to breathe; the midwest clings to me like a forgotten favorite sweater—one I lived in then but the fabric chafes against my skin now—somehow still smoke-soaked from almost decades distant nights of communion, of bonfires in the boonies, of boy-girl pair-offs. The smoke lives in my body...I can taste it, the pinewood tendrils curling eternally around my tongue, permeating my lungs, my cells. I inhale deeply and close my eyes. Nestled in the blackness in my periphery, little firecrackers languish too close by.

The girls I grew up with were slick
after Karyna McGlynn

& sweet as Splenda, saccharine, *four packets please*,
they soak you sickly until you forget it's bad for you

They had skin like frogs, elastic & moist, shedding
their bodies every weekend, not afraid to mislead you,
to try on another & another, catwalking brazenly
through the aisles of the Goodwill off of State Road 46.
They steered me down the highway of adolescence.

Converse & Matching Shirts & *We aren't talking to them*
today. They stepped down the halls silently & not without
pride, claiming the senior hallway every morning at 7:05
with a slouch like the high school itself was propping them up.

Their eyes glinted when they tossed quips, no hands needed,
instead fisting mickey d's frosties & fries from Arby's & when
one got get, banter dripping like Arby's sauce from the corner
of another's mouth, you could sometimes see their eyes strike flint.

They all took up late-night messaging, keeping watch for alerts
of alt lyrics & door creaks & rotating besties [pre/de]moted
on the daily. They had MySpace Top 8 & Bath & Body
Works sweet pea spray & intentions to be teachers & nurses.

Absent-mindedly, their tongues sliced at my folds, making pulp
of me. I was a blank page for them to write their stories on,
shoved into the corner of their backpack, tossed in their car.

I contorted myself into the little space remaining in their
Toyota Camry. I was eager & pliant & flexible & quiet.

& they didn't hear me—when the weight got to be too much
& they bore down too hard. They didn't listen for me at all.

Even though I'd learned all their favorite things & practiced
their subdued smile, the one that doesn't reach the eyes.

A Summer Day at Steak n' Shake, Indiana, 2006

My brother won't like what you're doing, not one bit—a phrase I've turned over, that has almost tumbled from my lips. Though I have no brother to call my own, the words wrap me with fizzy warmth, a kind of fleeting reassurance I've sought ever since he first rubbed his feet against mine at a restaurant with my best friend—his sister—sitting across from him. I wanted to walk away, outside the restaurant door, tear off my shoes and socks, hoping my brother would appear, ask what was wrong. Hoping he would tell him to *get your goddamn foot off*, that her brother would apologize to mine, *sorry, man, I didn't know she was your sister*. Because having a brother would warrant me an apology. Would make real my desire for him to stop.

.

.

Instead I stay and order a frisco melt on sourdough bread. The rain drips down the diner windows, despairing in my stead. Rain is a trickster, Puck incarnate. It's supposed to promise rebirth but offers only oblivion, and he offers me his coat and I don't want it and I don't take it but his sister—my friend—says, *why not? He's being nice, he's never nice just take it.* And so I hold out my hand.

His coat is a slow suffocation on the way back to her house. To his house. Her home is not mine, nor is her brother, and all the protections a brother seems to afford. I like a home with a front door that groans to announce your arrival. I like a home where you can smell that cooking and communing happens; it convinces me, just a little bit, that it is safer. I watch her mother clean the final debris from dessert off the dishes, wayward drips fall from the faucet. I watch her father extinguish the lights, flicking the final switch. And, even as I watch his sister shuffle up the stairs, I see him linger behind and think, *all over the city there are brothers and sisters. Any one of them could be mine.*

Towards softness

When I follow the line of follicles from my ankle down across my foot I feel warm. I hope it looks like fur. I hope in the summer when I strut in sandals, my thick strapped docs, that my little brown hairs thrive, that they sprout through and trail up and around and across my feet freely not unlike the distinct pleasure derived from friday nights in eighth grade that include hot tubs and slick secrets and cool cans of mountain dew—your friend crack-snaps one open and the moment shutters itself into some body-crevice where you tuck memories. You hide/hug this unexpected moment as he gets in close, like the words that slipped from his tongue as they traced their way down the warm brown fuzz of your, what, *happy trail*, he named haughtily, *nice*. Two days ago I stopped clearing the bristles of hair near and below my navel; now, they emerge unevenly and without care, unsmiling, tangled, taking the terrain anew and marking a growing season all their own. They are not soft but. nevertheless, they caress the curves of my stomach sensually, soothing the burning bumps that pervaded my skin prior, and claiming its own.

Arriving early means getting to watch the older girls

I have a dancing dream
hazy in the distance
one two three taps
toes feet slap

across the floor, I remember
rhythm, the beats, the hot hot hot
tunes as a cassette crackles,
a jarring click, rehearsal over,
sweat droplets all that remain
on the linoleum floor, our softer,
lighter, less practiced steps take
over, bodies sway, fingers grip
rainbow scarves, a colorful
spectrum of taffeta trembles,
fills the space their curves left
behind, I remember, yearn—

but all I have are others' words oxidized
hung out to dry in the dark, echoes of
my own pleasure, not unlike the scarves
swishing in the heat of what came before

The first time

I could love girls out loud, long-hug,
head to toe, body-sighs as we slip slide
retreat into each other's shoulder nook
after a long day—was in college, our house

sheltered 120 women. Here, we sleep together
in a large room, lights dark, to the soundtrack
of shared breath from bodies above and side
to side, we sign-up to wake each other every

morning, fingers gently pressing on another's
shoulder, whispering gingerly into her ear
It's time to get up and you don't want to be late.
We hold hands, we cuddle, we sneak-borrow

each others' clothes, swapping pheromones
like perfume and burrowing into other girls' laps
our skin electric, bodies charged, we power
one another. We take up space 3-4-5-6-7 to

a room modpodging its bones to buttress us. None
of the friends I found my way to after were in a sorority—
almost all of them queer, their bodies versed me in touch
as *yes* touch as *you are dear to me* touch as *I am here for you,*

and they traded touch vigorously, speaking care
without limits in the city of Philadelphia, of
brotherly love, of fraternity. When I set my sights
on state school, running hard and fast from Indiana

smalltown living, I knew I wanted to rush, to submerge
myself insatiably in the ambrosia of sisterhood. Sorority girls,
we had permission to touch, too, to love differently, to penetrate
the restraints tethered to each woman at birth, remake ourselves

with ribbon with glitter and glue and gaudiness, with garish colors
so showy so vibrant we split ears, you can't help but hear us.
This is ours. This we have devoutly crafted, painting each other
with powder like ardor, pouring into her cup, never letting it empty.

A pilgrimage towards friendship, queered

*I can't tell if I'm drowning or I'm floating so I just keep on going, going, and I'm
running just to hide and I'm hiding just to breathe and around every corner is the
same night on repeat.*
Sir Babygirl

Midnight.   My stoop calls me
to sit.   I   stumble over, pressing
end on yet another call unanswered.
I shouldn't have left her.   My   tongue
tastes salt steeping in humidity.   I swallow
the word   *mom,*   my fingers slipping   sticky
against my phone.   I'm alone   and   shouldn't be
but   I shorted the sense the city gave me, that it shouted
into my ears,   *She   shouldn't have left*

me.   Sound muffles into a ringing,   a tortuous tinnitus
tainting any approach of rational thought,   there's   only
my uncertain misunderstanding of where   I   am
tripping into my subconscious   until   a different ring—
your voice cuts the silence, static   slips   into my
ears   and   inbetween   coiling thoughts
and   everything   else   disappears, and I think
it might be nice to fill that new space with you.

Before therapy

*It feels so good to want things so desperately, that when you finally get them…you know
what you love with such certainty that it becomes how you make sense of yourself.*
Raechel Anne Jolie

There was Madeline.　　And I know　　I *know*　　the setup
sings romantic　　and it's not　　and it is　because isn't it　kind
of romantic to stumble upon　a person　who when you first speak to them
your breath gets tangled in your teeth　　your tongue tied so tight
it trips　shouting inside　　　*I know you* or　　*I need*

you—what's the difference really? One Sunday in Philadelphia—
yes, from *phileos* as in　　*dear* as in　　　*beloved* and *adelph[ē/ós]*
as in　sibling-family as in—I found you　　when I thrust the door open
into this windowless basement yoga studio, my eyes flicked　to Madeline
stuck to her I did not look away　I did not look away and we both mirrors

reflected.　This class　　this day　　this meeting, the steam and sweat
the pieces and parts of this hot yoga meet-cute　　saturate my mind,
the best class I have taken since—in a long while, and my invitation
after, *would you maybe want to get coffee sometime?*　I　clench
my business card, *is this an odd way to offer an email?* and Madeline

grins and says *yeah* or　*let's do it* or　　*that would be awesome* and pulls
out her card too. And it's not that I don't remember the words, which I don't
remember the words but mostly I remember that cling film feeling Madeline
wrapped me in　*yes* caressed me with　　*I'd love to*　　swathing us
in something more intimate　than the yoga studio could bear on its own

Did you know that carpal tunnel can cause your fingers to swell, changing longstanding ring sizes?

It is always evening, past midnight, and I have just hurried to zip off last emails and have just hurried to pack tomorrow's backpack and just hurried to update my phone to-dos and scrawl down some notes. When I fade into bed, you tuck the sheets around me and turn the lights on low, the fan on high. I send my hand long towards you—

I saw in a video recently that sticking your hands past wrist-deep in rice and rotating them slowly in one direction, then the other, can help develop wrist strength. It is best to do this, this slow swish swish of your wrists, while relaxing, while watching tv, while doing some sort of thing that gives you plenty of time to steep your wrists in these rhythmic rice rotations and build strength. Oh, you may feel soreness, they said, but endure…swish swish and strength will come.

—and your fingers embrace my wrists. Yesterday, I leaned my neck on my wrist, my palm on my head and tried to cradle my mind. My heartbeat thumped in my ears as my pulse rang from my wrists, but it wasn't louder than the warm ache-ache-ache that thrummed along with it. And tonight it is there and tonight you press circles, you make moons on my wrist and you aren't hurried at all.

New England Secrets

I walk into the barn, a solitary space suspended in time; *it could have been featured in a b-level horror film if it had any sort of structural integrity,* I muse to myself. It almost feels like a joke that I have trekked all this way to chase this spectre: a story I heard once, a barn I never visited and wasn't certain still existed, and that I am here all just to chase a ghost, my mother's ghost, the one my mother told me about seeing one time when she was twelve and limber and bloated with possibility—possibility now punctured. All I have is textures of a tale: my mom's fulfillment after finishing a long day's work, the magic of the minutes after midnight, of finding friendship in unexpected places, and a sudden, sharp sound accompanied by a sulfury smell like when fire first ignites. I remember this ghost occupied my mom's belly, the hearth of her spirit, and each time my mom uttered the tale, an ethereal mist crept from her lips, chapping them as it passed through, and lit stars in my mom's eyes. This was the intimate possibility of connection. All I want is to hold a piece of my mother inside me like my mother housed that ghost and to know that things will somehow end up okay, that magic might be real, that the inexplicable and unfathomable are tangible futures you can hope for. As the minutes edge past midnight, there is a sharp pop, a glistening something seeping in from the rafters, and in that moment I think, *maybe we are connected, maybe we are all made from all the same pieces and parts as our mothers and hold the potential to contain an extraordinary secret.*

Nostalgia Packed Tight

I splice open boxes in firm, intentional strokes, one after another, using the boxcutter my dad left behind. The rhythmic cracking and thwacking create an almost soothing meditation until I cut open the first box of books from a load my parents dropped off a week earlier—a pile of paperbacks peeks out at me that I prized in my teenage years. I pluck the first in the series from the heart of the box and thumb my way through; it smells like then. It smells like humid midwestern basements and sticky summers curled up binge reading in our papasan chair with a Mountain Dew, like the burnt-dust-flickering of clip-on reading lights that never stay adjusted right, the stale sweat of overheard fights, familial discomfort, words ill-thought-out and overrun and left unsaid. The spine sighs as I split the pages open to a favorite chapter—this book was my escape route of choice after my parents and I moved to our fifth state when I was eleven. This is the second bit of joy: being nuzzled by nostalgia in all of its complexities. I brush the tip of my thumbs across each page and I swear I feel something release, tickling the tightness from my shoulders, and dwindling to a warm whisper. My lips tug upwards. I look to my left and catch sight of the half-empty get-rid-of-it box at my feet: my partner and I's attempt to downsize our accumulated youth, which we only seem to get more of as we get older. My belly clenches, my own laughter catching me by surprise. *I'm a sucker for it: for the sentimentality and burst of brightness when you encounter an object familiar and beloved, a hoarder of feel-goods. It does make it harder and harder to move, but I've done it several more times and states since then.* I stop. And I wonder, for a moment, if this is subconsciously my goal, to cling to the feel-goods, afraid that if I rest, even for an instant, the feel-goods will scurry far, far away.

> Or, maybe, maybe it is to be able to have more
> moments like this, more frothy flirtations
> with the fragments of who I used to be.

The store is closed now

there is a soft sensation
a stinging-numb-tingling
that encircles my thumb
the phantom pulsations
reminding me to take off
my ring at night, to never
wear it too long, though
I never used to take it off—

I remember my mom lost
hers in the ocean several
years back, how crushed
and naked she felt missing
this circlet we delighted in
choosing out together in an
airport jewelry store, one of
the moments of mother-
daughterness where every
thing falls into place

—but last week I took it off, or
maybe it was the week before,
it became easier to leave the
band off than to coerce it over
my knuckle, to force it across
this newfound bloated barrier.
At least, that is what I whispered
to myself, what I repeated like
a spell when I tried to join her
back to me.

Loss upon returning home from visiting the Adirondacks with friends

In this poem curls a cat. She comes and curls herself to rest
on a woven yellow rug at my feet each evening. To clarify,
this rug is in my home and this rug is in the bathroom and
this rug is near the toilet, which is where I sit and why she

is nearby, a smile on her face and her pink-padded paws tucked tight,
waiting. And it is midnight. Or an hour past. Or sometimes, two. Because
late at night is when the next day nudges its way into my mind, swirling
its fingers amongst my lists of what not to forget and what not to forget and
what not to forget and I would much rather stay put than make my way
towards

the next day, which she knows and is why she tucks herself in
like a reminder: there is more to tomorrow than what you face alone
in your mind. She is curled up on this yellow rug much like how I settle
myself on my side when I sleep and in her little exhales are poems
of presence and love and lingering and patience. And when I do decide

to rise, when I tear my fingers away from my whirling worries and consent
to meeting the next day, she stretches in turn. She sits. She waits. And she
guides me into the bedroom with her tail aloft, constantly checking behind
as Orpheus wished to do with Eurydice but could not, lest he break
his promise and, through his own folly, permit her to disappear.
She checks anyway.

Her breathy poems promise some kind of sleepy sweetness and bid me
to bed as she leaves the yellow rug behind and turns and checks and turns
except, suddenly, when she turns around, when I imagine her turning, it is
not I who is gone but her. And I can't help but feel that I didn't keep
my end of the bargain.

Is this what catharsis feels like?

I send my legs long, striding steadily into the air. Ellipticalling is not my favorite exercise—I prefer group classes or outdoor runs so long I forget what worries are circling my mind. However, the pandemic has dictated many changes. The television flickers, this week's arbitrarily selected show snags at my whorling thoughts as its playful sentimentality pulls heat to my cheeks. Laughter. I feel light, effervescent at first, my body steady, flying perpetually forward. Continually advancing, ever progressing, until the sensation bubbles over. My body is flooded with an inertia that wracks at the box containing my exhaustion and flings my feelings about faster and faster until my body succumbs to my mind and it is a breathless collision—and by that I mean I have found myself wondering *what is it like to have an anxiety attack* and if it might feel like my body tangled in the throes of an elliptical, the sensation of a sob colliding with a gasp and a gasp and I can't quite catch my breath but isn't it awful? *What is happening on this show, at my school, in this country, in our world, in my head, in my head and in my body?* I leak thick, steady tears, which rival my rivulets of sweat, and that is saying something. But I am also saying to myself *on the elliptical, I don't let myself cry.* Oblivious, my legs continue to lunge forward unceasingly, latched into its large plastic footholds.

What facts, feelings, needs, or goals are in your head today?*

I have so many things to do   *I just want to go home*
my mom   started her second   round of a new   treatment
sometimes I think each day I choose to stay in another state is another
scar sliced into my heart, that in the future, I will regret my choice to chase
dreams and desires over purposeful proximity. Instead, the bulk of my time
is spent in the company of my thoughts, which are on indefinite lease by the
shouts and the worries of the so many things I have to do. And I just want to
go home. I   just   want to   go   home but if I were to relocate more
permanently, I fear I would regret not pursuing my dreams, which just reminds
me that I don't have enough time to do anything, I miss my family. My heart
hurts. I need a break. I don't want to go to work. I don't want to go to class.
And yet doing for students, being for students, makes me feel something.
I want them to witness playfulness, risk-taking, and authentic (appropriate)
vulnerability. I want them to feel encouraged to be their whole selves.
I drink two coffees before class every morning. And I perform. And
we play. And we check-in. I invite them to share what's in their
heads and what's in their hearts. And I see. And I'm exhausted.
I just want to cry, but I don't at the same time. I want school
to be over. I miss my [cat]. =(I'm sad. I miss my [cat]
again. =(It has been three days and six months since
I lost her; she was my best friend. I remember,
a few days after, I started teaching a new
class, which we began with rants and
raves. Her death was too much to
put on them so soon. And they all
have so much going on. *[They]*
just want to graduate already
and go somewhere warm.
But we are all just
too *busy.* We're
just too
busy.

*When I wrote this poem, I was in the midst of teaching undergraduate
students. This poem was written in witness and response to one of my
student's written reflections on their check-in (with
permission). The words in italics are the student's words.

Writing a daily medical note, at the request of my gynecologist

I am at the end of my fragmenting hands. I only have nerves to tell me how far.
Jennifer Militello

There has been a sharp pain in my left hand, a something pain

that is small, hot, a bullet, forcefully pushing, incising, a sharp circle
into my palm about an inch under my pinky. It pulses. It pulsates.

It has been happening and happening and happening without pause
for a minute. For two. When I push gently on the place,

the ends of my fingers start to go numb, the pulsations dance outwards
almost playful, like baby birds beaking. I am reading a book about
the body, about knowing. Jennifer Militello scraped

together a home in a corner of my mind, "Doctor, there are too many
nests for me." The pulsing pain has stopped, but the prickling

stars have claimed residence in my fingertips, not unlike
the childhood surprise of a friend fake-breaking an egg yolk across

your scalp, the claiming you, the spidery sensation, the yolk-you-
cannot-see.

Tendering the body

I want to know pleasure, to be her acquaintance, to be someone
on a first-name basis, the kind of knowing where she stays with me,
she stays and carves her initials onto the topography of my body,
a flourish finished with a heart and a fond *4 Eva*. I want to know
pleasure but   I defer.   All I can think about is the sensation
of showering,   of   slipping into   a   high
heat stream that courses across the terrain of   my body   kneading
the knotted ridges of my shoulders, a whirling column, surging
across the slopes of   my   side   stomach   and welcoming
the new folds of my belly in a way I have not made time for.

Phantosmia

There is bread burning. There was bread burning yesterday morning, in the hallway of our home. *Are you burning bread? Or making 'burnt toast'?* I jest. My partner stares, confused. Today, the burning bread rides shotgun with me in my Mazda hatchback, an uninvited guest on an ordinary array of errands—haircut, coffee and gluten-free donuts. She seethes. Her unseeable smoke tickles, taunts my nostrils with a kind of hostile hospitality and I freeze, flooded, on autopilot.But my body keeps moving through the motions, keeps anticipating what the car needs to navigate us to Strange Matter (an aptly named café—something strange is the matter with me). In so many ways, I am meeting my body for the first time. So many times, I wish I could render my body anew, sift her down to her basest grains, knead her, and let her rise again.

Writing the body

1. Collect your thoughts one by one, plucking them from the air around you, until you have enough matter to mold into something meaningful.
2. Decide what is meaningful today. Decide by pulling a three-card spread but if at anytime your thoughts start to swirl like a fish in a school, stop. They might spill over and distort the cards. Start again.
3. Find your body. Sink your sit bones into the floor. You need your body to be grounded. You need to be grounded in order to read the cards.
4. Make sure your school of thoughts is near your body, but not in your body. Palpate your abdomen, your throat, your jowls—is there a quiver? a swell wave? Take two fingers and scoop the school out fish by fish. Arrange the bits of your fish-bodies close to, but not touching, the cards in some sort of significant shape. The bits of your body deserve reverence. Return to the cards.
5. Fill your body with the images, the symbols, the meanings of the cards, setting them alight one by one and pressing the remaining pulp into the grooves of your molars. Exhale. Glow.
6. Feed the glow with your thought-matter, the luminescent pulp, the bits of your fish-bodies, until you have consumed the whole school and are glowing profusely.
7. Reach your other hand deep into your mouth-gut. Your wrist may ache. Catch the glow.
8. Thread it through the eye of your leaden needle. Don't forget your needle. It's heavy. Lift it anyway.
9. Pull. Coax. Stitch. Embroider the haze to your head, the aches at your hinges. Secure the swells. Steadily
10. Until you have secured the outline of your body, the fiery stitches shining softly as you, struggling, point, and flex, and point your foot again.

An ode to fish pose

which I step into feet first every
Thursday, clinging to the high-low
table in my chiropractor's office as it sends
my upper body long towards
the floor, head resting below my heart.

To the *oohs* and *ohs* and the *yeah,*
that feels okay, to the sudden intake
of air, to the big belly breath and the
extended exhale that comes after,
sizzling across the ridges of my teeth.

To releasing the aching the burning the
cramping the diffuse; the dull, excruciating
numbness; the pounding, pulsating, radiating,
sharp-shooting-stabbing-stiffness; the throbbing;
the tingling-tightness, the weakness, the ascension.

To the crack of relief that comes when
I make a snap decision, letting go
of the control I've been death-gripping,
wiggling my toes until—the thwack of
release, shoulders inching lower, wider,
heart shining upwards. My throat opens.

Body Memory

Sometimes at night my thoughts
wander to a friend I haven't
spoken with in years but who
I loved briefly and   intensely
and I feel the tear, an acidic
aching near the left pocket
of my chest, a cavity where
I made a souvenir of/from myself
wrapping it with a whisper, *Tuck*
this away, carry me, display
me, and it keeps me up at night,
the breeze from the window unit
catching the hollows of my skin.

How do you put fanfare into a poem?

When I walked into the classroom, they were already enmeshed with one another like a zipper threaded tightly on a jacket. Did you all do this? I crooned. The answers assent and range in intensity. I had walked from one place still tuning, trying to locate my middle c but ringing flat, and suddenly it's brassy and bold—I'm bold—I strut to literal applause across this runway scaffolded, zippered, by their hands. Bellows of recognition tune me true: I'm back at middle. There is something about an orchestra being assembled, finally all back together after a wintering apart, that is rich and needy and affirming. I have a secret, my body chirped. I came by Friday to check this place out before we gathered here today, and it was just dreadful. No chairs, but rigid desks? I flopped into one for dramatic effect. My body wailed exaggeratedly, how will we even get comfortable? And I laughed. We are a we again. And we laughed, hitting tones and timbres all our own.

I. The summit of my physical body/ Page of Pentacles, Reversed

I am intimately acquainted with yearning, with a body-
ache so deep, a fascination of the world so fluid
that I can't stop my body from reaching, fingers quivering
forward to collect the next thing and the next
with no account for the capacity my bones can bear, and
as the bits of my curiosity accumulate, I feel a break,
my focus fuzzes, sinew stinging, but I don't stop
seeking bodily productivity, don't stop climbing
the stairs before me—instead, I stumble upwards, against
the protests of my body, my focus waning. The vantage shifts
to something stranger, less familiar. You looked away from me,
from my physical body, from the imprint these chronic illnesses
have started to make. Your eyes are closed, but I know you
are looking away. I think, *maybe I am overwrought, maybe*
I shared from my own body too soon and too often. From this
vantage, I start to see what you do, too.

II. In seeking compassion/ Ace of cups, Reversed

When I was younger, I briefly balleted—my body remembers:
my teacher, envisioning our hips as goblets, directing us, *imagine,*
your hips, your pelvis, carry a bowl of water that you must contain—
ah ah ah don't spill! Drop your tailbone down, balance it. Balance
it. Don't find a fake turnout, and don't spill the water! It turns out,
my left leg is a fraction of an inch shorter than my right; I learn this
when I suffer an injury to my piriformis, several years after
I set my slippers aside.

It prickles persistently still, diffusing down across the back of my hips,
decorating the unstable bowl of my sacrum with cords woven
from bruised purples and blush reds. I stand, the crack-pop of my
body calls me back to this moment, needing movement to moisten
its palette, to nurture the new growth rings resting heavy on my hips.
I extend my own cup forward cradled strongly by my capable hands,
my blessed body, and I think *this cup is full enough*, but it isn't. There
is a leak. I don't know where, but I know it's there, coiling its course
through my body, waiting to make itself known.

III. Room to improve/Knight of Swords, Reversed

Standing in the bathroom is hard
for me now. There are two mirrors
that sit at just-under-hips-height and
extend beyond the crown of my head,

and I hesitate to meet my own gaze,
hesitate to see the shifts that are documented
across the skin sitting at my midline—and it is not
my newfound stretchmarks I stall in meeting

head on, but their way of speaking to me, of speaking with
my body. I don't speak their language. I thought I did, but
I don't. My body is trying to tell me something and I can't read it,
can't trace its appeal for healing to the source of the flares, and I feel
like a fraud, an imposter, wearing out her welcome.

IV. In seeking connection/ Strength, reversed

I clench my toes, grounding my grip in the coarse shag of the cut pile carpet. A lock pulls loose, a souvenir from the first day when getting up feels like too much. *What can I do from here?* I don't reply to the seven unread text messages on my phone. I don't mute the alerts pinging from my work email, my personal email, my second work email. I don't close my eyes. I want to. I want to rest. I want to embrace the sensation slowly and wholly and for this to be the beginning of me sitting with revolution in a room with my body. I want to be formidable. But I'm afraid. There is no amount of rest that can recover my body from the throes of its unmapped needs.

V. Grounding myself/ Four of cups

This summer, I don't set an alarm most days. I want this to feel nice. I want this to counteract my waking up one, two, three times a night, every night. I want this to feel-good away the sour dreams that simmer on low when I do fall asleep. In the mornings, when I decide to stop shutting my eyes, usually sometime around eight, I oscillate sensations — switching off the window AC, saturating, switching on the window AC, an incessant groaning [from the AC—not me], and, finally, switching it back off when I can't swim through the sounds any longer. Neither the sweat nor the sound drowns out the permanent construction zone that has made a home in my head or the nausea niggling at my gut. Waiting can be disappointing, it can be a blur of unfeeling and feeling all too much, at the same time.

VI. My spirit wants/ The lovers

I haven't been able to crunch
into an apple for months, slurp its
juices from those endearing to-go pouches,
make an impromptu decision to trek
ten minutes and dig into a chunk of apple pie—

I don't eat them and I wait in a kind of stasis,
a purgatory of misunderstanding as apple-picking
season approaches—-a must-do in Michigan. My body's
pain is more than apples. It's a gnawing around the stem
that persists whether suspended from a tree, sheltered by
a hand, or bolstered by the sturdy base of a basket.

It is the fog that arrives at the orchard off-season, confounding
climate scientists as it descends, impenetrable, when all
the orchard thirsts for is for someone to take a closer look
before the harvest.

A room of our own

They moved like a single organism—or, rather, a single collective mind. A hive of
girls. A swarm of women. A murmuration of dancers. They threw their heads back in
ecstatic joy.
Kelly Barnhill

Hands clasped, sweaty and tight, we eagerly entangle
ourselves in each other in that way only girlhood
garners, a distilled knowing that this is not friendship

but fierce fellowship, a once-in-a-lifetime fondness
that thrives best in buried places, in the forest where
the alarms sounding in our heads are finally silenced

and we dress in all the ways we would worry and warn
ourselves not to otherwise, if we weren't here, gossamer
gowns made filmy from our merriment, our joy reverberates

as we toss toasts side to side, and if you were to step back
and look, you would see that pleasure pulses across our bodies,
inseparable from our collective consciousness, and that if you wish
to fly, to be lifted into your own, you only have to extend a hand.

NOTES

"The girls I grew up with were slick": This poem is after Karyna McGlynn's "The Girls I Grew Up with Were Hard" in *50 Things Kate Bush Taught Me About the Multiverse* (Sarabande Books, 2022).

"A pilgrimage towards friendship, queered": The epigraph for this poem is from Sir BabyGirl's "Haunted House," which is on his album "Crush on Me" (2019).

"Before therapy": The epigraph for this poem is from Raechel Anne Jolie's *Rust Belt Femme* (Belt Publishing, 2020).

"Writing a daily medical note, at the request of my gynecologist": The epigraph and citation in this poem are from Jennifer Militello's poem, "Autobiography Toward a Study of the Thousand Wounds," which is in her collection *Body Thesaurus* (North Adams, MA: Tupelo Press, 2013).

"A room of our own": The epigraph for this poem is from Kelly Barnhill's *When Women Were Dragons* (Doubleday, 2022).

Brittany Brewer (she/fae) is a queer & chronically ill poet, [theatre] artist, and educator who researches and writes plays and poems whose aesthetics sing of sticky, midwestern basements, of stumbling queerness, of female friendships and sexuality and bodies, and of the magical possibilities that exist in the in-between. She is an alumna of Indiana University, Brown University, and the Arden Professional Apprenticeship program. Currently, fae is a doctoral candidate in Curriculum, Instruction, and Teacher Education at Michigan State University where her research focuses on the intersections of poetry and playwriting, arts as research, embodiment, young adult narratives, queer theory, and arts-based feedback practices. Her scholarly writing appears or is forthcoming in the Journal of *Adolescent & Adult Literacy, English Journal, The Reading Teacher, The Northwest Journal of Teacher Education,* and *Intraspection* among others. Before MSU, Brittany worked as the Associate Director of Education at Philadelphia Young Playwrights where, among other things, fae facilitated over 315 classroom workshops and created/facilitated professional development workshops for classroom teachers, teaching artists, and classroom actors. As a playwright, Brittany's work has been produced by Revolution Shakespeare, Going Viral Festival, Elephant Room Productions, and Allens Lane Art Center. Faer poetry has appeared in *Rougarou, Months to Years,* and *Hole in the Head Review,* among others. Most recently, she was awarded a Workshop Fellowship to attend the Key West Literary Seminar Writers' Workshop in early 2024. For more: www.brittanybrewer.com

www.ingramcontent.com/pod-product-compliance
Lightning Source LLC
Chambersburg PA
CBHW022057080426
42734CB00009B/1386